Latinos in the Limelight

Christina Aguilera   John Leguizamo

Antonio Banderas   Jennifer Lopez

Jeff Bezos   Ricky Martin

Oscar De La Hoya   Pedro Martinez

Cameron Diaz   Freddie Prinze Jr.

Scott Gomez   Selena

Salma Hayek   Carlos Santana

Enrique Iglesias   Sammy Sosa

CHELSEA HOUSE PUBLISHERS

LATINOS
IN THE
LIMELIGHT

John Leguizamo

Amy Allison

CHELSEA HOUSE PUBLISHERS
Philadelphia

Frontis: John Leguizamo, vibrant star of stage and screen, has made a name for himself as the first Latino to produce his own one-man Broadway shows.

CHELSEA HOUSE PUBLISHERS

Editor in Chief: Sally Cheney
Director of Production: Kim Shinners
Production Manager: Pamela Loos
Art Director: Sara Davis
Editor: Bill Conn
Production Editor: Diann Grasse

Layout by
21st Century Publishing and Communications, Inc.
http://www.21cpc.com

The Chelsea House World Wide Web address is
http://www.chelseahouse.com

First Printing

1 3 5 7 9 8 6 4 2

Library of Congress Cataloging-in-Publications Data

Allison, Amy, 1956-
    John Leguizamo / by Amy Allison
        p. cm. — (Latinos in the limelight)
    Includes bibliographical references and index.
    ISBN 0-7910-6477-8 (alk. paper)
      1. Leguizamo, John. 2. Dramatists, American—20th century—
    Biography. 3. Comedians—United States—Biography. 4. Hispanic
    Americans—Biography. I. Title. II.Series.

    PS3652.E424 Z54 2001
    812'.54—dc21
    [B]   2001028085

CONTENTS

FREAK

Broadway—the mecca of the American theater world. Actors fantasize about one day starring in a show in this famed theater district in the heart of New York City. On opening night on Broadway, a performer feels at the top of his or her career.

February 12, 1998, was such a night for John Leguizamo. On that night the 33-year-old stage, film, and television actor made his Broadway debut. He also made history. No other Hispanic performer before him had ever produced his own one-man show on Broadway.

Freak, subtitled "*A Semi-Demi-Quasi-Pseudo Autobiography*," introduces audiences to a Latino immigrant family struggling to make it in America. John explains the show's title, *Freak*, this way: "It's the story of not fitting in, being an outsider, feeling freakish wherever you go." He adds, "Mostly as an adolescent you feel that, and that you have to overcome things." In *Freak*, John narrates his own story about coming to terms with his identity and arriving at the brink of an acting career.

In his autobiographical one-man show, *Freak,* Leguizamo portrayed nearly 40 different characters, telling the story of the Queens, New York neighborhood where he grew up. After proving a hit on Broadway, *Freak* was produced as an HBO special on cable TV.

"Hopefully, this is going to be the most dangerous work I've done so far," John said about creating *Freak*. "It's hard because it's embarrassing and painful."

The pain and embarrassment came from the more personal direction this play took than John's two previous, off-Broadway shows. He confessed to the *Los Angeles Times* that performing the piece "felt like some kind of fun-house mirror of my life." When his mother came to see *Freak* he recalls that she cried for days afterward. "Developing this show was a speeding train, and I couldn't find the brake. It was fun at first till I got reactions from my family; then I realized, oops," he says.

Highlighting the personal thrust of *Freak* is the show's final image: a blown-up snapshot of John and his father from when John was a boy. The play tackles John's rocky relationship with his father head-on. In one scene, the actor flies across the stage and bounces off the curtain frame to simulate his father throwing him against a wall.

Although Alberto Leguizamo comes across as a drunken bully in *Freak*, John insists his portrayal is a compassionate one: "My father was a product of the immigrant experience," he explains. "I placed him in a context and showed just how hard he struggled and how many times he was crushed."

For his part, Alberto, now a success in the real estate business, called the press to protest his depiction in *Freak*. He denied he physically abused John and John's mother and younger brother. At that point, he hadn't seen or spoken with John for a couple of years. Then one night after receiving a standing ovation following his performance, John

found a visitor in his dressing room:

> I see this shadow, and then I see this scowl, and it's my father. I turned white and he's beet red and he's foaming at the mouth and he waits till everybody leaves and he says, 'How dare you! Is this what you think of me!' He says it twice 'cause he's dramatic. And then he runs out of the theater and I chase him and he runs into his Lexus . . . and we drive around and I yell at him and curse him and tell him all the things I never said to him, and then he cries and we hug and I feel amazing, like the world knows everything and sets you up like its puppet and pulls your strings 'cause everything is kind of for a reason.

John's reconciliation with his father reached a high point when Alberto accompanied him to the Tony Awards celebration in June 1998.

In 1998, John Leguizamo became the first Hispanic performer to produce his own one-man show on Broadway. The play, *Freak*, was a semi-autobiographical story about being an outsider. In it, John shared from his experiences with family struggles and the start of his acting career. Here he is arriving at opening night.

John's performance in the HBO special *Freak* earned him a well-deserved Emmy Award in 1999.

People who work in American theater consider the Tony the ultimate recognition of their work. *Freak* received nominations for Best Actor as well as Best Play. Later filmed as an HBO special, the show would earn John an Emmy in 1999—television's highest honor—for Outstanding Performance in a Variety or Music Program. Meanwhile, as another measure of its success on Broadway, *Freak* played to sold-out theaters for nearly six months and had its run at the Cort Theatre extended twice.

The raves he won for his performance onstage in *Freak* landed John on *Entertainment Weekly*'s "It List" for June 19, 1998. "With his remarkable elastic face and expressive body,

Leguizamo can turn an action as simple as a child's effort to hide a broken television aerial into comedy that is at once stunningly complex, hilarious, and awesome to behold," reported *The San Francisco Examiner* when *Freak* premiered in that city, before its run at the Cort. Nine months later, when *Freak* reached Broadway, *The New York Times* observed that John's metamorphosis into the play's characters seemed "less an act of impersonation than an instance of possession. There's a whole city of people inside this young man's slender frame."

The "city of people" the *Times* referred to is none other than the Jackson Heights, Queens, section of New York. Recalling his arrival as a child in the neighborhood, John transformed onstage into an entire community—one moment he'd be an Indian candy salesman, the next a Korean newsstand owner.

In fact, throughout the one hour and forty-five minute show, John would morph into nearly 40 different characters. "With a flick of his shoulders and a heave of his chest, he goes from Irish to Italian, Indian to West Indian," reported the *Village Voice*, astonished at "a persona so plastic it can cross genders in a flash." In the same scene, John might carry on four- and five-person dialogues without any noticeable transition from character to character. Shortly after the start of the show, for example, John launched into a surreal recounting of his birth, playing everyone from his mother in the throes of labor to his impatient father and the frazzled doctor.

John inhabited all these characters on a bare stage with no costume other than a shirt and slacks and no prop except a tall stool.

Along with the actor's dynamic presence, a lively musical score made up for the starkness of the set. Salsa, mariachi, and hip-hop music were interwoven through John's narrative. John's preparation for the show actually included taking break dance lessons—and practicing his moves at New York City clubs.

Performing *Freak* did make more serious demands on John's life. Doctors ordered strict vocal rest for the actor offstage. Thus, throughout the run of *Freak*, John spoke only during performances. He and his girlfriend communicated by sign language. When interviewed, he'd type out his responses on a laptop computer. "I carry cards that say, 'Thank you,' 'I can't talk,' and 'When do I get paid?'" John joked at the time.

Despite the sacrifice, John reveled in his acceptance on Broadway. "It's great because theater is really important to me," he told *Los Angeles Times* journalist Patrick Pacheco. "That's what I used to learn about life and to educate myself." He gives as an example learning the word *mendacity*, meaning "untruthfulness," from Tennessee Williams's *Cat on a Hot Tin Roof.* He'd use the word at home until his father bellowed, "Shut up and go to your room till you can speak like normal people."

As a tribute to his love of theater, John recreated in *Freak* his reaction to seeing his first Broadway show. Playing himself at 17, watching the show, John would leap into a box seat in the audience of *Freak*. The show he recalled himself watching, *A Chorus Line*, featured a Hispanic character named Morales. Turning his face, aglow in the spotlight, from the stage back to *Freak*'s audience, John would say, grinning, "And everybody was watching her." Then, after a pause, he would

add: "The way you all are looking at me."

Echoing his excitement at seeing a Hispanic character onstage, John says that kids in *Freak*'s audience have told him "they feel so inspired by the show that they wanna be actors, writers, directors. That my making my own thang, shows them that they too can make their own thang." John stresses his need to "follow the beat of my drum." He adds, "It's not about the awards or the reviews or the audience liking me. It's about creating what I need to say."

John actually calls *Freak* his very own "emancipation proclamation"—the pain of revisiting his early life offering a sense of liberation. "Because now, anything that happens to me can't be as bad as when I was growing up," he explains. Indeed, the shattering of his parents' immigrant hope of living the American dream marred John's childhood years.

After a performance of John's Broadway hit, *Freak*, he is congratulated by fellow celebrities, Demi Moore and Madonna.

CLASS CLOWN

2

"**I** was born in Latin America," John says. "I had to—my mother was there." John credits his mother for not only his place of birth but also his first name. Luz Leguizamo named her firstborn after her favorite movie actor, John Saxon. "The worst B-movie actor!" John laments.

John describes Luz as an exotic-looking woman. Native American, Arab, Spanish, and possibly Jewish and African blood run through her veins. Attractive and with plenty of suitors to choose from, Luz married Alberto Leguizamo. Evidently Alberto's cultivated, worldly air gave him an edge over his competitors. Alberto had acquired his apparent polish in Europe.

At 19, Alberto had left Bogotá, Colombia, for Italy with ambitions of becoming a movie director. After two years of apprenticeship at Cinecittà, one of Italy's great film studios, Alberto returned to Bogotá. Now 21, he lost no time in marrying and starting a family. John was born on July 22, 1964, followed by a second son, Sergio. "Having to bring home the Kraft macaroni and cheese put an end to my father's cinematic aspirations," John says.

Throughout his career, John has sought to broaden the range of roles and acting opportunities open to Latinos. Even when forced to take negative roles, he says, "it's better to be seen than not to be seen."

Other ambitions took their place. In 1966, Alberto and Luz immigrated to the United States in hopes of a more prosperous life for their new family. While their parents found work and saved money to make a home for them, John and Sergio stayed behind in Colombia with grandparents. Then, when John was four, he and Sergio joined Alberto and Luz in the city known as the Big Apple: New York.

The family settled in Queens, a borough, or section of the city, in a working-class neighborhood called Jackson Heights. "All the peoples of the world stop there before they go on to wherever it is they have to go—Irish, Italians, Jews, Puerto Ricans, Dominicans, Chinese, Greeks, Colombians, Ecuadorians." True to the immigrant dream of a better life, the Leguizamos, too, strove to leave Jackson Heights behind.

Alberto found employment as a dishwasher, then as a waiter and occasional landlord. Luz labored in a doll factory and also worked as a bank receptionist and a Hamburgler at McDonald's, passing out fliers in a black-and-white-striped prison outfit. Putting in long hours on their respective jobs, the couple was hardly ever at home. Much of the time, John and his brother were on their own.

Left to care for his little brother, John "inflicted all sorts of torture" on Sergio. "I was a mad [Dr.] Frankenstein and he was my monster," John confesses. "I often made him taste things no human being has ever tasted—or ever will." The boys had to rely on their imaginations for amusement, since they had no toys. "There was no money," John explains, "and toys to my parents were like some bizarre waste."

The Legiuzamos did, however, own a television set. Gathered around the set, the family, who fought a lot, enjoyed rare moments of closeness. John would imitate the characters on the shows, making his father laugh. "It was like an oasis would appear where these little pockets of affection could come out." Mostly John remembers being scared of his dad. "He was strict and hypercritical," Johns recalls. "He was like a machine."

Alberto seemed driven to succeed. Luz, for her part, wanted something more for herself and her family than a hand-to-mouth existence. Starting out, the four Leguizamos shared a studio apartment, with just one tiny room and a bed that folded into a closet. But, because of the determination of John's parents to get ahead, the family moved constantly, to someplace bigger each time. Eventually they had their own house. "Unfortunately, all the rooms but one

When John was only two, he moved with his parents and brother from their home in Colombia to the Queens, New York neighborhood of Jackson Heights. John's parents took a variety of jobs to help support the family in New York, but these commitments meant they were rarely at home with the children.

were rented out, so we had to live as if we were in a studio again," John recollects.

His parents' efforts to prosper suffered a major setback when John was eight. Alberto and Luz had invested much of their earnings in electronic goods and furniture. They had planned to sell these at a profit in Colombia, allowing them to enjoy a comfortable life there. The family arrived in Bogotá only to discover the merchandise stolen—along with their personal belongings. Again the family separated. John's parents returned to New York City to start over, and he and Sergio remained in Colombia with a grandmother.

Within a year the two boys were reunited with their parents in Queens. That summer and for the next two summers as well, John got a break from the crowds and pace of the city. In a program sponsored by a nonprofit agency, the Fresh Air Fund, John was sent with other city kids to the countryside of Vermont and New Hampshire. "I used to watch *The Brady Bunch* and be jealous because they had this big house and yard—all the normalcy I didn't have. So when I went to the Fresh Air Fund, I was like, 'Oh, my God, I got my own Brady Bunch!'" John says.

After being away for the summer, John headed back to New York—and the classroom. Because his family moved so much, John attended a lot of different schools. As the new kid in class, he had to make new friends every year. "You never get really comfortable," John says of the dislocation he felt, "you're always trying to find yourself."

Life grew even more chaotic following his parents' divorce when John was 13. Alberto and Luz's bickering intensified to the point that one night, Luz gathered up the two boys and left. "All that struggling, disappointment, all that being crushed just destroyed my parents' relationship," John reflects, adding, "but it was liberating in a lot of ways for me." Living with his mother, he was free of his father's hard-nosed authority.

More changes lay ahead for John in high school. Starting out as the class nerd, he reinvented himself as the class clown. As John tells the story:

> My mother used to buy me Nucons, these sneakers that are like $1.99, and I had high-waters, too. Everything was cheap. For six months, this one guy made fun of me all the time. The whole class would laugh, ahhahaha.
>
> One day, I just couldn't take it. I took the guy down into the subway, threw off my jacket and beat . . . him. . . . I didn't realize I had so much rage pent up inside of me. . . . Pretty soon I was coming in every day and making fun of *him*, and people were laughing. Then I spent the whole four years, the rest of high school, making people laugh. I'd found some source of power.

The budding performer started writing jokes at night, then trying them out in class the next day. The attention proved addictive. "When the teachers would crack up and laugh with me, it was like breaking down my parents," he reveals. But all too often John's antics spun out of control. He remembers spending most of 10th grade in the dean's office.

In fact, John's high jinks got him in more serious trouble than a trip to the dean's office. Once he was arrested for truancy. He and some buddies cut class one day and were caught

John's mother, Luz Leguizamo, left her husband when John was 13, taking her sons with her. After a rocky period during high school, marked by troublemaking and arrests, John enrolled in college and began to focus on acting.

trying to sneak into an adult move theater. The student voted "Most Talkative" by his high school class also ran afoul of the law by talking back to a cop. He faced arrest, too, for jumping subway turnstiles to avoid paying the fare.

Another brush with the police also involved the New York City subway system. John and a friend broke into an empty conductor's booth on a subway train. Turning on the public address system, they announced themselves as "your new subway deejays." Launching into a comedy routine, they subjected startled passengers to such jokes as "How do you catch a squirrel? Climb up a tree and act like a nut."

Their "act" lasted four stations along the subway route. Then suddenly the pranksters found themselves handcuffed and carted off to the police station. "I was shaking like a human vibrator, quaking with fear," John says. "My mother comes. She's crying, 'He's my little angel! How could you do that to my angel?' And I start crying because she's crying!"

Alarmed, John's parents packed him off to Colombia for a year. They hoped that reconnecting with his roots would dispel the restlessness that made him so wild and unruly. Instead he chafed under exile from the excitement of New York City. Back home, John resumed his troublemaking. "Juvenile delinquency was my goal," he deadpans.

At 17, John's disruptive behavior—including locking a teacher in an elevator—threatened to get him expelled from Murray Bergtrum High School. He agreed to enter therapy at the city-run Youth Counseling League. Sessions at the League helped him calm down. Says John, "Therapy made me appreciate myself."

Also during John's senior year, his high school math teacher, Mr. Zufa, urged him to try acting and standup comedy. "You're very funny. Do something with it, instead of getting into trouble," John recalls Mr. Zufa telling him.

John thought about what Mr. Zufa had said. The teenager recognized he had problems, low self-esteem, and an uncertain future. Flipping though the telephone book Yellow Pages, he spotted Sylvia Leigh's Showcase Theater. With three hundred dollars he had earned working at Kentucky Fried Chicken, John enrolled in act-ing classes taught by Leigh.

The eager young student threw himself into learning his craft. His mother remembers that John would lock himself in the bathroom and practice his characters for hours. John's new focus transformed him. "If acting hadn't come along, I'd either be a doorman or be in jail," he says.

Early on, John had looked ahead to an exciting future as "a freedom fighter or a forest ranger." Plenty of adventure definitely lay ahead for him in his newest ambition: a career in show business.

MAMBO MOUTH

John wasted no time in pursuing his dream of breaking into show business. Right out of high school, he auditioned for Julliard, which offered one of the most famous acting programs in the country. His rejection to the program cited his thick New York accent.

Disappointment switched to hope, however, when John returned home from the audition. A phone call from one of the judges encouraged him to stick with his dream of an acting career. Further rejection awaited, however. John failed to gain acceptance into another acclaimed drama program at New York University (NYU).

Instead, he enrolled at C. W. Post, located in Long Island, New York—"the least competitive school in America," according to John. "They'll take anyone, anytime." Determined to excel, John made the school's dean's list. Then, in his junior year, John was able to transfer to NYU.

Finding himself the only Hispanic student in his drama classes at NYU, John claims that at 19 he became "a born-again Latino." He determined then and there to make theater and film a place to explore Latin culture. Growing up as a Hispanic-American, he says he "felt like an invisible person—

Before getting his first job as an actor—a small role on the 1980s TV show *Miami Vice*—John worked a series of jobs, from busboy to salesman, but never lost sight of his goals.

like all our aspirations, all this joy, this experience, this contribution to America, didn't count. Nobody documented it. I felt a longing to create a legacy, a memory about surviving, about people who made it against the odds."

Driven to succeed by "that immigrant mentality in my blood," John signed up for acting classes outside his program at NYU. Besides the legendary Lee Strasberg, John's teachers included Wynn Handman, who trained, among others, Oscar winner Denzel Washington. "My inner Geiger counter immediately told me: 'This is an extraordinary talent,'" Handman says about John's audition to take his class.

While still enrolled at NYU, John appeared in a student film, *Five Out of Six*. His performance in the award-winning project caught the attention of casting director Bonnie Timmerman. Her connection to the television cop series *Miami Vice* led to John's three appearances on the show in 1984. "We liked John so much that we killed him off once or twice and still found ways to bring him back," says Timmerman.

Playing Calderone Jr. on *Miami Vice* was John's first paying job as an actor. He remains conflicted, if unapologetic, about the role. "*Miami Vice* gave so much work to Latin actors. And every Latin actor wanted to be on it because it was exciting. It was filling our pockets and destroying us at the same time. It perpetuated so many negative stereotypes. Unbelievable. Every Latin man was a drug dealer. . . . But it's better to be seen than not to be seen," he reflects.

Three years after his television debut, John dropped out of NYU. He had believed that he was about to graduate, but he discovered to his dismay that many of his credits from C. W. Post weren't transferable.

Eager to continue performing, John joined Off-Center
Theater, a children's theater
company. "He got onstage
and just stayed there," recalls
Abigail Rosen, the company's
creative director. "We needed a
broom just to get him off."
John himself remembers writing jokes in order to "juice up"
his parts in plays at Off-Center.
His Jack in the Beanstalk, for
example, "was a scam artist
who tried to rip off the giant."
He adds: "No other acting job,
before or since, has given me
so much satisfaction. The kids
enjoyed it almost as much as
I did. Inspired by their honest
and uninhibited responses, I
couldn't control myself and
ended up stealing every scene."

In the thriller *Whispers in the Dark,* John played a painter who puts fantasies on canvas.

John now counted himself among the many
struggling actors in New York City. He supported
himself—barely—with a variety of jobs. These
included working as a busboy at a Mexican
restaurant and as a salesman at a clothing
store. He also cleaned apartments. Another job
involved reading textbooks to a legally blind law
student. "I would try to act it and he'd say to just
read it plain and fast," he recollects. "I fell asleep
reading the books a couple times."

John's big break seemed to come when he
landed a part in the movie *Casualties of War.*
The part was that of a sensitive young soldier
caught up in the savagery of the 1960s war in
Vietnam. The role of Diaz was John's first ever in
a Hollywood film. As a bonus, he got to work

with an idol of his, Sean Penn. "He was the young actor who was [the] most daring, " John says. "From Sean I learned that acting is real and you can let it go as big as you want." According to John, Penn—who played John's troop leader in the movie—remained in character all during filming. He even made John do 25 push-ups whenever John said something wrong.

Despite expectations, the 1989 release of *Casualties of War* didn't do much for John's career. The only offers that came his way were for token Hispanic roles. John lists these roles as "drug dealers, gang members, thieves, crooks, all this underbelly stuff." In *Revenge*, starring Kevin Costner, he appeared as a Mexican bandit. In *Regarding Henry* he played a mugger who shot Harrison Ford. In *Die Hard II*, with Bruce Willis, he was cast as a terrorist. "My part was so small there could be a trivia question: How many times did Leguizamo flash across the screen in *Die Hard II*? It's seven times," John jokes. More seriously, he said at the time, "It's hard to say whether I'm on the verge of a break. I really do believe that things would be different if I were a white guy."

Faced with the limited options Hollywood offered Hispanics, John determined to create his own opportunities. "The only way to change things is to write and be in control of projects," he concluded. In fact, he was already creating his own material in New York comedy clubs.

It was while performing in a club in 1986 that John met fellow comedian Carolyn McDermott. The two ended up dating and were even engaged for a while. They also teamed up briefly as an act. With John a full four inches shorter than McDermott at 6' 1", the couple drew stares. "I met her when she was sitting down so I didn't know how tall she was," John deadpans.

Eventually the demand of comedy club audiences for nonstop, rapid-fire jokes frustrated John. Instead, he wanted to create characters and stories. Inspired by the solo stage shows of actor-comedians Lily Tomlin and Whoopi Goldberg, John began developing characters for a one-man show of his own. "I feel it's the oldest form of storytelling," he says of the show's monologue format. "It's the first man . . . sitting around the fire . . . and retelling the day's events and acting them out."

John tried out his characters in Wynn Handman's acting class. Sitting in class one day, a directing student of Handman's named Peter Askin saw John perform Pepe, an illegal immigrant from Mexico who was trying to talk his way out of being deported. "What stood out first, second, and third of all was his acting," Askin says of John's performance. "Plus he was Hispanic and dealing with what that meant, through original material."

Throughout the summer of 1990 and into the fall, Askin worked with John in shaping his character pieces into a full-fledged show. On November 8, *Mambo Mouth* debuted in the small, 74-seat Sub-Plot space at Handman's off-Broadway American Place Theatre.

By the play's opening, John and his costume changer, Theresa Tetley, had the breaks between character monologues down to a minute. Costume changes took place behind a scrim, or semitransparent screen, at the back of the stage. Silhouetted against the scrim, he and Tetley played out scenes leading into the monologues. Tetley, for example, mimed a cop walloping John as the leather-jacketed Angel Garcia. Garcia then half swaggered, half staggered onstage, handcuffed, with a bloody nose.

Angel was one of seven characters John

In his controversial one-man show, *Mambo Mouth*, John challenged the media images of Hispanics through a series of exaggerated characters.

inhabited during the show. Another was Agamemnon, a super-macho host of a public access television show. "In his own little world, Agamemnon's a star," John said of the character. "He's fighting to keep it together. That's where the strength to me lies. I always feel like Latin people are trying so hard against so many odds." He added: "I want Latin people to leave with a sense of pride, saying that no matter how down we are, we can overcome anything."

Not all Latinos had that reaction. Coco Fusco, a female columnist for the *Village Voice*, accused John of perpetuating Latino stereotypes. "[D]on't people see that I'm mocking Latino men, their macho attitudes?" John countered. "Don't they see this show is an exorcism, a purge, of all the media images of Latinos? Can't they see that I'm saying we should stop all the self-hating that goes on in the Latino community?"

He argued that the show used humor as a weapon against feelings of inferiority. "[Y]ou've got to be strong to make fun of yourself," he said. "In creating *Mambo Mouth*, I felt that mocking the Latin community was one of the most radical ways to empower it. I love the world I come from, and only because I do can I poke fun at it."

As for accusations that *Mambo Mouth* encouraged Anglo audiences to scorn its Hispanic characters, John said he aimed 80 percent of the show directly at Latinos. As a matter of fact, he insisted on using Spanish in the monologues. John also cited the support of most of New York's Latino press for the play.

In ticket sales at least, the public voiced its approval. Demand for seats moved *Mambo Man* to the American Place's mainstage in February 1991. After packing audiences in for a total of six months, *Mambo Mouth* closed at the American Place Theater. It then reopened, again off-Broadway, at the Orpheum Theatre. There it ran for 12 weeks, from June to August, 1991. Of John's performance, *The New York Times* declared, "[L]ike Eddie Murphy at his best, he communicates with the audience a shared sense of reveling in his sheer, overflowing talent."

Presenters of the OBIE Award, the off-Broadway equivalent of the Tony, agreed. John scored an OBIE in 1991 for his performance in *Mambo Mouth*. The play also won John the Outer Critics Circle Award for Outstanding Achievement. By receiving this award, it meant that writers on New York theater from all over the country singled out John for recognition. In addition, American playwright greats Arthur Miller and Sam Shepherd visited John's dressing room to congratulate him on the show.

The success of *Mambo Mouth* propelled the twentysomething performer out of the minor leagues of show business and into the majors. The release of *Hangin' with the Homeboys* in 1992 reinforced John's new-found celebrity. His first leading film role, as a nerdy clerk, won him praise in *The New York Times* as "an actor of virtuosic range." John would continue to demonstrate that range as he went on stretching himself creatively. Before *Mambo Mouth* ended its run, the energetic performer was already at work on a new stage show.

HOUSE OF BUGGIN'

Nearly six months into performing his hit show *Mambo Mouth*, John felt restless. He was eager for a new challenge. Then one day he noticed a guy in soldier fatigues hanging out at a New York street corner, carrying a boom box. Imagining what the guy's life might be like and remembering friends in the service, John started improvising a new character. The character, a veteran of the 1991 Gulf War named Krazy Willie, was finding the transition to civilian life difficult.

Other characters emerged from improvisations John built on Krazy Willie. These characters made up the Gigante family: mother, father, three brothers, and a cousin. "The family is where it all begins. It's what forms and drives us for the rest of our lives," John explained about his choice of subjects for his new project. "Some of the most important theater works, masterpieces, have been about families." As examples, he listed as his two favorite plays: Eugene O'Neill's *Long Day's Journey Into Night* and Arthur Miller's *Death of a Salesman*. "So I set out to create a comic tragic family that is closer to the way I perceive the world," he continued. "Sort of funny and painful at the same time."

From stand-up comedy to comedic monologues and dramatic roles, John's exuberance and talent have made him a favorite of audiences in film, theater, and TV.

John's work-in-progress about the Gigante family followed the monologue format of *Mambo Mouth*. But rather than writing random sketches, John wove the monologues together with a common theme: preparing for Krazy Willie's wedding.

Before opening his new play in a theater, John tried it out in several New York clubs, three or four monologues at a time. His brother, Sergio, often helped him carry costumes and equipment across town. Previewing parts of the show in small, lesser-known performance spaces allowed him freedom to experiment and revise. He resolved to nurture and develop the piece apart from the harsh glare of the media.

Indeed, a series of rewrites followed these early previews. At the same time, John was preparing for the physical demands of performing a one-man show. "I started running daily and working out like a fiend. I needed the aeorobic endurance for this 105-minute show that could last even longer, depending on the laughs," he says. "And I had an ulterior motive—I wanted to look good in Gladyz's [one of the characters] tights and midriff."

Along with spandex, Gladyz Gigante wears huge earrings, spiked heels, and bright red lipstick onstage. "Gladyz can talk, she can dish," says John of the character he based loosely on his own mother. According to John, Luz Leguizamo is a strong woman who taught him an important lesson in life: "to embrace and be open to every experience."

In the play, Gladyz runs the model laundromat for her husband Felix's Laundryland franchise. The play features the immigrant, lower-middle-class Gigantes, and is "about the discount dream you get when you come to this country,"

Never shying away from controversy, John's play *Spic-O-Rama* opened to packed houses in Chicago. Although the title offended some Hispanic Americans, John was determined to bring his characters to life on the stage, and the show's popularity soon overwhelmed any negative press.

John says. "You get the laundromat instead of IBM." He originally planned to call his new show *Discount Dreams*.

The title John finally settled on, *Spic-O-Rama*, sparked a lot of controversy. (Spic is an offensive term for a Spanish-American.) John painfully recalls being taunted with the term when he was nine years old. Still, he defended his choice. "I'm not just gonna write what's safe. That would be stupid and boring," he said. "I *like* the title. I think it's real funny and provocative."

John argued further that the title raised a battle cry where Latinos are shamefully under-represented—that is, the media. "I figured I'd use a title that screamed, 'Hey, someone's ignoring us,'" he explains.

Its title did cost *Spic-O-Rama* some viewers. Without having seen the show, some news stations in Chicago—where the play premiered—refused to publicize it. Despite the controversy—or maybe because of it— *Spic-O-Rama* played to sold-out houses during its two-week run at Chicago's Goodman Studio Theatre. "[A]lter-nately hilarious, scathing, and heartrending satire," reported the *Chicago Sun-Times*. "One of the season's sensations," proclaimed the *Chicago Tribune*.

Chicago theatergoers were still clamoring for tickets when *Spic-O-Rama* moved to the larger, 400-seat Briar Street Theatre on January 27, 1992. The play sold out its first two weeks and was extended another two weeks. Closing day, March 15, was declared John Leguizamo Day in Chicago.

Months later, in October, *Spic-O-Rama* opened off-Broadway, at New York City's Westside Theatre/Upstairs. John had offers to take the show to Broadway. But that big break came with strings attached. John would be tied to eight performances a week for a minimum of six months. He figured all he could endure physically was four months at six performances a week.

After all, the demands of performing *Spic-O-Rama* left him drained and hoarse. Starting to prepare at 3 P.M. for an 8 P.M. start time, he'd end up with a raspy voice and burning throat by the close of each performance. John also wanted ticket prices to be affordable for lower-income people. Broadway producers balked at such conditions.

Eventually, John himself signed on as one of the producers of the show. "I was scared," he admits, since "the chances of getting my money back looked grim."

But not for long. Previews played to packed houses. Then the reviews came out. The New York *Daily News* applauded *Spic-O-Rama* as "acidly funny." *New York Newsday* called it "compelling." The show was so hot, Madonna came to see it, her entourage in tow. *Spic-O-Rama* easily sold out its four-month run at the Westside.

Consequently, John's investment in the show nearly doubled. This success was especially sweet for the actor, since he had invested money that he had "painfully earned" for his part in the film *Super Mario Brothers*. John had shot the film in the months between the Chicago run and the New York premiere of *Spic-O-Rama*. He charges that nothing came of the film producers' promise that he could add material for his character, Luigi Mario. "There have been times when people cast me and then all of a sudden they just squash who and what I am and flimflam me. And it's just like, 'What's the point? Why didn't you get somebody else? I'm not that flat, boring character,'" John says.

The actor's disappointment in *Super Mario Brothers* was borne out by the film's failure at the box office—despite it's being based on a popular video game. A romantic relationship between John and costar Samantha Mathis fizzled as well.

John's experience on *Carlito's Way*, a crime drama shot in 1993, couldn't have been more different. He felt liberated by director Brian De Palma's encouragement of ad-libbing on the set. "That was the first time I ever had total fun on a film," John recalls. "I felt that people trusted me and my work and what I could do."

With the freedom to improvise, John created a Latino film character that defies stereotyping. John managed to reveal a sense of dignity in the villainous drug dealer he played. In fact, John lists the role of Benny Blanco as one of his favorites. The character showed "a different side of me," he explains. "It's a more serious and aggressive and assertive side."

John's next major project had him again going for laughs. He signed on with HBO Independent Productions to create a sketch comedy series for television. Executives first offered John a series following cable station HBO's 1991 broadcast of *Mambo Mouth*. However, they wanted a situation comedy, and John couldn't see himself in a show "where everyone's nice and lovable, PC, cute, and boring." This time, HBO Independent Productions president Chris Albrecht simply asked John what he wanted to do next. The answer: a comedy-variety series.

"It was a dream I had since I was about 20, to have a sketch-comedy show with Latins in it and Latin themes, and to just show the world how funny Latin people are, how witty and clever," recalled the then-31-year-old performer. John believed so strongly in the project, he turned down film roles to make it happen. "I made this choice because this was where I could make my life count a little more," he told *Entertainment Weekly*.

The choice made John the first Latino since Desi Arnaz in the 1950s (with *I Love Lucy*) to star in, cowrite, and coproduce a prime-time television series. The title of the series, *House of Buggin'*, John defines as "a place of craziness, of

The first prime-time Latino sketch comedy show, Leguizamo's *House of Buggin'* premiered on Fox TV in 1995, featuring a cast hand-picked by John himself. John was so committed to the project that he even paid for extra writers out of his own salary.

true freedom." John explains that whenever he acted crazy in high school—which he frequently did—people would go, "John, man, you bug!"

Also true to his roots, John lobbied hard for the show be taped at a studio in Queens, New York, rather than in Hollywood. John considers New York City "The Capital of Latinness." He says, "[Y]ou can't get this flavor anywhere else, man. You walk in the street, people yelling, and screaming, people telling the truth all the time."

John's insistence on authenticity didn't stop at where to base the show. For five months before *House of Buggin'* taped for television viewing, John performed live with his hand-picked cast at local New York clubs. Soldiering together in the trenches of comedy clubs forged a strong bond among cast members. John hoped this bond would produce the kind of chemistry that made comedy troupes like Monty Python so thrilling to watch.

This and other ambitions John had for the show didn't come cheap. Each episode carried the relatively high price tag of $700,000. The investment was particularly risky because unlike sitcoms, variety shows generally lack syndication value. That means they rarely recoup their cost with reruns. Still, John's commitment to *House of Buggin'* was total. He paid money out of his own salary for extra writers.

HBO Independent Productions, for their part, expressed their commitment to John. "John is as talented a person as I've ever worked with," said HBO's Chris Albrecht, a former agent of, among others, Eddie Murphy and Jim Carrey. "He's carrying forth a voice to the public that hasn't been heard before, and that's what makes him so exciting. It's not just the sheer talent that makes it exciting; it's exploring previously uncharted territory."

On the very first showing of *House of Buggin'* in 1995, that risky territory included such sketches as John in a blond wig and British accent advertising "illegal alien makeovers." Offended by the idea of an Anglo-European standard of beauty, a Hispanic rights group in California threatened to boycott the show. John fended off the threat by releasing a statement clarifying that the sketch satirized the makeovers. As a matter of fact, five of the six-member *House of Buggin'* cast were Latino. When *House of Buggin'* premiered on Fox-TV, on Sunday, January 8, 1995, from 8:30 P.M. to 9 P.M., it made history as the first prime-time Latino sketch-comedy series ever.

The same week the show premiered, a group of 45 Hispanic organizations announced a boycott of ABC-TV. The boycott protested a lack of Latino representation on network television. The group singled out ABC among the networks because of a broken promise to hire more Hispanics.

John spoke out in support of the boycott. "ABC and all those other channels have to get the pulse of America and find out what's going on because, you know, we're here," he said in a news conference. "We're $190 billion of buying power."

The success of *House of Buggin'* proved there was an audience for Latinos on television. The night it premiered, the show boosted the network's ratings 20 percent for its time period. After three airings, it drew a number 2 rating in 32 markets nationwide, including New York City, and a number 1 rating in Los Angeles.

Still, as the television season wore on, *House of Buggin'* failed to capture a big enough audience to satisfy Fox. At least not to justify the show's expense per episode. Fox very likely factored into the cost the hard time the writing staff (including John) gave the network censors. For his part, John was convinced that removing tough topics and talk from the show stripped it of its street-smart attitude. Whatever the ultimate reason for its cancellation, Fox pulled the plug on the series after just 10 episodes.

But if John's skills and talents seemed to overpower the small screen, the big screen offered them sufficient space. The actor now turned to movies to showcase his high-voltage performance style.

MORPHING MAN

In his television series as well as his one-man shows, John appeared before audiences dressed as a woman. Not surprisingly then, the producers of *To Wong Foo, Thanks for Everything, Julie Newmar* tapped him for a role in the film. The 1995 release follows the adventures of three men in drag—that is, masquerading as women— embarked on a cross-country road trip.

At first, John turned down the part. Because he'd done drag before, the actor didn't feel it offered him much of a challenge. Nevertheless, the film's director, Beeban Kidron talked him into taking the role. How? She promised, John says, to let him go "wild and crazy." With Kidron's blessing he got to ad lib lines for his character, for example, "We were so poor, my parents got married for the rice."

John describes his *To Wong Foo* character, Chi Chi Rodriguez, as a "little street urchin" being groomed by more sophisticated cross-dressers, played by Patrick Swayze and Wesley Snipes, "into a full-fledged diva." High-spirited and flirtatious, Chi Chi is also tough and determined.

Asked if he would date a person like Chi Chi, John replied, "I don't know if I could handle someone like my

---

Inspired by a comic book John loved as a kid, the film *Spawn* featured John as the 400-pound villain, Clown. Each day, John waited over three hours while artists applied the character's make-up and costume.

character. I need a little more peace at home." John was in fact married at the time. He met his wife, Yelba Osorio, in an acting workshop in 1991. "I thought he was kind of shy," recalls Osorio. "But he looked good in racing shorts." The two ran off and eloped in the summer of 1994, during filming of *To Wong Foo*.

The character of Chi Chi would appreciate this bold, romantic move. A male who believes he's truly a female, Chi Chi longs to find a knight in shining armor and live happily ever after. When a sweet-natured young man in a small Midwestern town begins falling for her, Chi Chi must decide whether or not to tell him the truth.

To play Chi Chi's scenes with her male admirer convincingly, John had to go beyond his own sexual preferences. He says he had to "find the innocence of being in love for love's sake." Kidron notes, "The bridge John crosses [in the role] is from stand-up comic to actor." Indeed, playing Chi Chi earned John a Golden Globe Award nomination for Best Actor in a Supporting Role.

Beyond praising his performance in the film, critics commented that John looked prettier than his costars. A rivalry actually did spring up between John, Patrick, and Wesley. "I've never heard women be competitive about their looks the way these three guys were," the film's female director told *People* magazine. The rivalry sparked a near fistfight between John and Patrick, stopped only by "the pregnant director sticking her belly between us," John recalls.

Make no mistake, John suffered for his beauty. He had to wear padded bras that were so tight that he ended up with skin burns. And

walking around on high heels caused corns and bunions on his feet. What gave John the greatest discomfort, however, was the daily removal of his body hair. During the movie's three-and-a-half-month shoot, he shaved his legs, arms, and chest, as well as his face, up to six times a day. He never got his eyebrows back completely from all the plucking.

John got so tired of the primping, he was eager to follow up *To Wong Foo* with "something really aggressive and stunt-like." That turned out to be the action-packed *Executive Decision.* In the film, John plays a member of an anti-terrorist team assigned to rescue a hijacked plane. Heightening the film's suspense, the plane is carrying a deadly nerve poison onboard.

But John soon tired of the action formula. "I wanted to do something a little more intellectual," he explains. So he signed on as a cunning, fast-talking agent in *The Fan,* a

For the film *To Wong Foo, Thanks for Everything, Julie Newmar,* John played the role of a drag queen, along with co-stars Patrick Swayze and Wesley Snipes. Although John had at first turned down the part, the director's promise to let him ad lib his lines finally convinced Leguizamo to take the role.

thriller about an obsessive fan of a baseball star. Of his own fans, John said at the time, "They always call me by the character in the movie. When you're chameleon-like and not just playing your personality and people know the character, that's a big honor—that they really believe those characters are real."

John's chameleon-like abilities in front of the camera not only made him a more marketable actor, but also challenged the typecasting of Hispanic performers in Hollywood in general. John's career was evidence that a Latino actor could play a broad range of roles.

John liked mixing it up not only with the kinds of parts he took, but also with the scale of the films he appeared in. He enjoyed doing big-budget films like *Executive Decision* and *The Fan* as long as he could balance them with more intimate, serious-minded films. Acting in such films, he said, while "emotionally painful," does "make you grow."

John definitely got to stretch his acting muscles in a movie adaptation of *Romeo and Juliet* starring Leonardo Di Caprio and Claire Danes. Guns and gangs and hip-hop music update this version of Shakespeare's tale of ill-fated love. The filming of the classic tragedy was itself beset with difficulties. Along with illness and injury, the weather on location in Mexico plagued the cast and crew. John recalls trying to do a scene with a sandstorm raging through the set. "Cups of sand are like in your eyes. You're like 'Thou wretched . . . Where are you?'" he jokes. Such setbacks aside, John treasured the experience of working with director Baz Luhrmann.

"Baz brings out this passion in you to do better. To strive." John says. Indeed, John's

performance, as Juliet's vicious cousin, crackles with electricity. His snarling fury as Tybalt powerfully dramatizes the hostility between the feuding Montague and Capulet families.

In 1996, the year *Romeo and Juliet*, as well as *Executive Decision* and *The Fan*, was released, *Boxoffice* magazine described John as "striding to the verge of major stardom." He also was headed for divorce. In divorce papers filed in November, John accused his wife, Yelba Osorio, of kicking and scratching him. Also, John claimed, Osorio wasn't satisfied with his efforts to help her acting career, though he cast her in his television show, *House of Buggin'*.

The following year, 1997, John's personal life changed for the better. He started dating Justine Maurer, who is not in show business.

In an updated film version of William Shakespeare's classic play *Romeo & Juliet*, John played Tybalt, with guns replacing swords and a hip-hop soundtrack backing his performance.

Meanwhile his professional life continued on an upswing. In 1997 came the release of the highly anticipated film—costarring John—of the cult comic book *Spawn*. Featuring a superhero that cartoonist Todd McFarlane first came up with in high school, *Spawn* quickly became America's best-selling comic book.

"I loved doing *Spawn* because the comic book is the bomb," John says. "I loved comics as a kid, and I'm still a big fan."

And while he normally finds clowns annoying, John liked the villainous Clown character he played in the movie. "This one's like a regular little New York thug, and I had a lot of fun with him," John says. The fun included a prank he played on some trick-or-treating kids on Halloween. Bored while waiting to be called to the set, John left his trailer and wandered onto the street, looking hideous in his costume and makeup. Sneaking up on the trick-or-treaters, he yelled "Boo!" They screamed. One kid tried to hit the frightful clown with his Tonka truck.

At 400 pounds and 4' tall, Clown was not a pleasant sight. John, who's about 5' 7", had to crouch low to drop to the character's height. After crouching a long time during an extended take, John would sometimes collapse once the director called cut.

Adding to the demands of the role was the three and a half hours John spent in the makeup chair every day of the shoot. With his hair slicked down and a latex hood glued over his head, John's face was first covered with a mix of acrylic paint and some material to make the paint stick. Then it was airbrushed. Next he was put into a 20-pound "fat suit" with foam latex hands. John remembers staring at himself in the mirror in his trailer and wondering, Who am I? What am I?

About John's transformation, creature effects artist Howard Berger said, "We were a little skeptical at first because he's a little guy and we were going to have to build up so much rubber it was bound to be tough on him. It can get scary because it really inhibits your movement. But we had forgotten who we were dealing with. John made the character that much better because he's such a great performer. The whole thing comes alive with him."

Sweating and itching uneasily in his Clown getup his first day on the set, John wasn't sure exactly how he would get into the character, he confesses. "[B]ut the guy said, 'Action,' and my voice got all gravelly and I started spitting and hissing and squatting really low, and I got a round of applause." John clearly was earning his $2 million salary as the wisecracking evil Clown.

The next character John played, while not a fiend like Clown, was certainly no angel. Pestario Vargas is fittingly nicknamed "Pest." In the 1997 film *The Pest,* Vargas sees himself as a great con artist. John admits the character is a bit like himself, "heightened to my most annoying, crazy, zany, mad, manic self . . . like a thousand beans of coffee turned up volume-wise."

John came up with the character with his buddy David Bar Katz, who explains, "John is extremely lovable and a really nice guy, but he's also constantly doing shtick and provoking people. He's a little troublemaker and that's Pest's defining attribute."

To carry out his scams, Pest pretends to be many different people. This allowed John to play a lot of zany ethnic characters in the film. John's experiences growing up helped him portray an almost international cast of characters. He recalls walking down the block in his Queens,

John describes his character "Pest" as a Latin Bugs Bunny. The role of this lovable troublemaker allowed John to play many different characters.

New York, neighborhood and hearing all kinds of accents. "I always had a sense of otherness, of other characters and other people, and I appreciate the dignity people have. So when I try to do my characters, I don't try to do stereotypes," he says, though he admits, "sometimes characters aren't as tridimensional as they could be."

In fact, John describes Pest as a Latin Bugs Bunny, and he plays the character more like a cartoon character than a recognizable human being. The performance shows John's love of slapstick, or broad physical comedy.

Another love of John's—for animals—had

him doing one of his own stunts for the film. The script called for a 6' snake to crawl up Pest's bare leg. John insisted on doing the scene himself rather than using a stunt man. When the scene stopped filming, the snake got upset at being removed from John's thigh. So it bit him. Then it wouldn't let go. Its fangs had to be removed at a hospital.

John's desire to do a lot of improvising on the set didn't end up as he had planned, either. According to screenwriter David Bar Katz, the script for *The Pest* served solely as a starting place for the film. That is, it laid down some "solid scenarios" for the actors to develop physical comedy bits around. This gave John a chance, Bar Katz adds, "to do what he does best: play on the set."

Such an improvisatory approach, however, requires filming eight or nine takes as opposed to the usual two or three for each scene. On a project like *The Pest* with a limited schedule and budget, the improvisation eventually had to be cut back. John blamed such constraints for the film's later flopping at the box office. "You can't compromise your vision," John said in summing up the lesson he learned from the experience.

"Films don't really capture the essence of who I am," John said. So he was determined to get "back to what really fulfills me as an artist." So he headed back to the stage in a one-man show. This time his name would be in lights high above Broadway.

6

HEART ON FIRE

The success of John's 1998 Broadway show *Freak* strengthened his commitment to forego Hollywood stardom and celebrity in favor of doing his best possible work. "I want to be more selective, and do projects that are more fulfilling for me. I want to do the quality of work I go for in theater," he told journalist Shashank Bengali.

The fact is, John's chances of fulfilling his ambitions remain limited in the American film industry. Big-studio Hollywood movies tend to be, in John's words, "giant amusement rides." That is, they're mass-produced for mass consumption. Banking on the tried-and-true, they routinely typecast performers and expect them to portray stock characters or stereotypes.

According to John, the "saving grace of American cinema" is the independent film movement, which operates outside the big-studio system. "That's where everyone can take more chances," he explains.

To support efforts by actors as well as writers and directors to take risks onscreen, John and colleague David Bar Katz started their own their own production company in 1996. They even located the company—Lower East Side Films—outside Hollywood, in New York City to be exact.

While hosting the Yahoo Online Music Awards in 2000, John used his comedic skills to help celebrate the most revolutionary artists on the internet.

John chose to premiere a coproduction of Lower East Side Films, *King of the Jungle*, at the first New York International Latino Film Festival, held in October 2000. He was eager to support the festival, believing strongly in its promotion of Latino actors, directors, writers, and producers. He applauds efforts by the Latin-American community to organize and have its voice heard. His mother, after all, is politically active in the community and visits inner-city schools to give inspirational talks as "Johnny Leguizamo's mother."

John himself avoids a leadership role in Latin-American political efforts. "I don't want to take on a false responsibility, something that isn't me," he says. "What I can do is show the Latin image—the savviness, the intelligence, the brightness, the wit of it—through my films." He adds, that means "controlling the project on all levels. The uniqueness of a voice comes through a lack of bureaucracy, otherwise . . . you get a commercial product." Productions by Lower East-Side Films go the distance in living up to that ideal.

Ensuring the integrity of *King of the Jungle*'s point of view, its writer, Seth Zvi Rosenfeld, also directed the film. John stars as Seymour Weinstein, a half-Jewish, half-Puerto Rican mentally challenged young man. John researched the part for months at a home for mentally challenged children. He wanted to avoid "a shallow portrayal that's embarrassing to them," he says. "I tried to find myself in there and I think the thing that they have that's beautiful is truth in emotion. I tried to find that in myself."

John didn't shirk his research, either, for his work on the 1999 film *Summer of Sam* for controversial filmmaker Spike Lee. The suspense drama looks back more than 20 years to the summer of 1977, when New York City was

terrorized by a mysterious killer known as the Son of Sam. John was 13 years old that summer. "There was paranoia," he recalls. "Lovers' lanes were empty. I used to bike there all the time to see if I could learn something—you know, through all the fogged-up windows. But there wasn't anything. It was creepy."

Beside drawing on personal memories, John prepared for the film by watching television news clips about the Son of Sam's reign of terror. He also spoke to cops assigned to the case. In addition, he and costar Mira Sorvino took dance classes together to help create the chemistry of a married couple.

John credits director Spike Lee with the sense of camaraderie he and his costars felt on the set of *Summer of Sam*. He explains that Lee encouraged the actors to rehearse and hang out together. According to John, Lee's approach resulted in more truthful acting, since cast

In the Spike Lee film, *Summer of Sam*, John co-starred with Mira Sorvino, dramatizing the way the Son of Sam murder spree of 1977 affected a Brooklyn neighborhood. To prepare for the role, Leguizamo and Sorvino took dance classes together to help create the chemistry of a married couple.

members felt so relaxed with one another.

In fact, the *Washington Post* declared John "wholly believable" in his starring role as Vinny in the film. Similarly, *Variety* praised the actor, along with *Summer of Sam*'s other leads, for being "entirely convincing as working-class types struggling with their lives just as they feel their very existence threatened."

Beyond the critical praise for his performance as Vinny, the role was a triumph against type-casting for John. A Hispanic actor was playing an Italian-American character in a reversal of the Hollywood norm. Throughout its history, Hollywood has cast Italian-American actors as Latinos.

Despite their different ethnicity, John and his character Vinny shared working-class roots as well as the ordeal of the summer of '77 in New York. While John could look to his own experience to guide his performance in *Summer of Sam*, his role a year later in *Titan A.E.* pushed him to the far reaches of his imagination. The character he voices in the animated film is a turtle-like alien named Gune.

John saw Gune, who navigates a third-millennium spaceship, as a kind of goofy little mad scientist. So he created a spooky, breathy voice for the character, similar to that of Peter Lorre, an actor in classic horror and suspense films. "Leguizamo's sometimes grating, high-pitched voice is almost unrecognizable," noted *Variety* in its review of the film.

According to *Titan A.E.* codirector Don Bluth, John's endless creativity showed in his many different recordings of the same lines for Gune. Codirector Gary Goldman, for his part, was impressed with the actor's skill at timing his voice-over readings. Goldman noted that John read his lines with the intuition of an animator.

Bluth and Goldman, as well as the film's cast and crew, faced a huge challenge on *Titan A.E.* They had just 18 months to complete the ambitious project. The film's two-dimensional hand-drawn characters occupy a spectacular three-dimensional computer-generated world. The achievement of its creative team was recognized by *Titan A.E.*'s nomination for an Annie Award, handed out by the animation industry. The nomination came despite *Titan A.E.*'s disastrous showing at the box office in summer 2000.

John's voice-over talents were also enlisted for the live-action Nickelodeon television series *The Brothers Garcia*, which premiered in 2000. John provides the voice of the now grown-up Larry Garcia. From a witty adult perspective, the actor narrates Larry's efforts as an 11-year-old to get along with his two older brothers and be independent from his twin sister.

As the first English-language sitcom with an all-Latino cast and team of writers, directors, and producers, *The Brothers Garcia* is, John says, "long overdue." He remembers growing up watching *The Brady Bunch* and never seeing a Latino on television except "on the news—as a villain." He adds: "It's really important for kids to see [a happy] Latin family." Ordering 13 more episodes of the series in October 2000, Nickelodeon stated that the show's strong ratings proves "kids' dreams and concerns are universal and cross all cultural bounds."

John took a flying leap across cultures on another television program seen in 2000. That year he appeared in the lavish ABC miniseries *Arabian Nights*. John remembers learning as a child some of the stories in the classic collection. "They always grabbed my imagination," he recalls.

Here's John arriving to host the 2000 Yahoo Online Music Awards.

In the story of Aladdin in the miniseries, John portrays both the sleek, serpent-like lamp genie and his distant cousin, the chubby ring genie. It took John nearly four hours to be transformed by makeup artists into the ring genie. He says he vowed when he did *Spawn* never to put himself through such sessions in the makeup chair again. "I had some sort of short-term amnesia," he explained about taking the role.

John also suffered in the hands of makeup wizards for his role as the height-challenged

French painter Henri de Toulouse-Lautrec in the movie *Moulin Rouge*. "[T]o make me short they came and put this [sadistic] contraption on. So I look short but have little tiny ankles that move. It's killing my knees and my back," he revealed during the shooting of the film in May 2000.

The device, however uncomfortable for the actor, allowed for historical accuracy in portraying the famous artist. When he was an adolescent, Toulouse-Lautrec broke both of his legs and they failed to grow properly. Still, his deformity didn't stop him from becoming a major figure among the free-spirited poets, artists, and entertainers gathered in Paris in the 1890s. *Moulin Rouge* revisits their colorful world.

Director Baz Luhrmann approached the project with a boldness true to the film's convention-defying characters. Luhrmann sees *Moulin Rouge* as nothing less than a reinvention of the musical film. Because of complications caused by the movie's soundtrack and musical score, *Moulin Rouge* was pushed from a Christmas 2000 release date to summer 2001.

John is set to appear in another high-profile film in the summer of 2001. *Collateral Damage* stars Arnold Schwarzeneggar as a man on a mission to avenge the death of his wife and child by terrorists.

John's personal life has also been progressing. John's girlfriend, Justine Maurer, gave birth to the couple's daughter, Allegra Sky, on October 24, 1999, in New York City. The following year, on December 5, 2000, John and Justine welcomed a baby boy, Ryder Lee, into their family.

The family lives in John's four-story town-house in New York's Lower East Side. The townhouse features a large graffiti painting, woolly white rug, and zebra-print upholstery.

The American Latino Media Arts (ALMA) Awards were created to honor positive portrayals of Latinos in film and TV. In 1999 John received two ALMA's.

Architect Steven Harris says, "The design is pitched at a certain level to accommodate a fairly chaotic and creative lifestyle."

John's desire to express himself creatively remains a driving force in his life. "I wanna do things that are my innermost dreams . . . and I don't want anything to get in the way," he's said. So it's my life's work never to care an ounce for anything anybody says except what I feel inside."

Indeed, John has avoided playing it safe, performing in dramas as well as comedies and portraying historical as well as contemporary and even mythological characters. John has said that the tattoo on his right shoulder serves as a reminder "to dare. To risk." The tattoo shows a heart being stabbed and set on fire—and still living. To John the symbol says, "No matter what, I'll survive."

CHRONOLOGY

1964	John Leguizamo born July 22 in Bogotà, Columbia
1968	Joins his immigrant parents in New York City
1984	Enters the drama program at New York University; appears on the television cop show *Miami Vice*, his first paying job as an actor
1987	Drops out of NYU
1989	Makes his feature film debut in *Casualties of War*
1990	Premieres his first one-man show, *Mambo Mouth*, Off-Broadway
1991	Wins an OBIE Award for his performance in *Mambo Mouth*; his second one-man show, *Spic-O-Rama* premieres in Chicago at the Goodman Studio Theatre
1992	John Leguizamo Day declared March 15 in Chicago; *Spic-O-Rama* opens off-Broadway at the Westside Theatre/Upstairs
1993	John wins Cable ACE nods for performing and writing *Spic-O-Rama* for HBO; the show takes an ACE as Best Comedy Special
1994	Marries actress Yelba Osorio
1995	*House of Buggin'* premieres on Fox-TV and is canceled after 10 episodes; John receives a *Golden Globe* nomination as Best Actor in a Supporting Role for his performance in *To Wong Foo, Thanks for Everything, Julie Newmar*
1996	Divorces Osorio; starts Lower East Side Films with David Bar Katz
1997	Earns a $2 million paycheck playing Clown in the live-action film of the cult comic book *Spawn*
1998	Debuts on Broadway in his one-man show *Freak*; receives Tony nominations for Best Actor and Best Play
1999	Wins an Emmy Award for Outstanding Performance in a Variety or Music Program in the HBO production of *Freak*; becomes a father for the first time when daughter Allegra Sky is born October 23
2000	Hosts My VH1 Music Awards on November 30; son Ryder Lee born December 5

ACCOMPLISHMENTS

Film

1989	*Casualties of War*
1991	*Revenge* *Die Hard 2* *Street Hunter*
1992	*Hangin' with the Homeboys* *Out for Justice* *Regarding Henry*
1993	*Whispers in the Dark*
1994	*Super Mario Brothers* *Puerto Rican Mambo* *Carlito's Way* *Night Owl*
1995	*A Pyromaniac's Love Story* *To Wong Foo, Thanks for Everything, Julie Newmar*
1996	*Romeo and Juliet* *The Fan* *Executive Decision*
1997	*Spawn* *A Brother's Kiss* *The Pest*
1998	*Doctor Doolittle* *Body Count* *Frogs for Snakes*
1999	*Summer of Sam* *Joe the King*
2000	*Titan A.E.* *King of the Jungle*
2001	*Collateral Damage* *Moulin Rouge* *What's the Worst That Could Happen?*

Television

1984   *Miami Vice*

1991   *Mambo Mouth*

1992   *Spic-O-Rama*

1994   *House of Buggin'*

1997   *Freak*

2000   *The Brothers Garcia*
         Arabian Nights

Stage

1990/1   *Mambo Mouth*

1992/3   *Spic-O-Rama*

1998   *Freak*

Awards

1991   Outer Critics Circle Award for Outstanding Solo Performance for *Mambo Mouth*; OBIE Award for Performance for *Mambo Mouth*

1992   Lucille Lortel Award for Outstanding Achievement Off-Broadway for *Spic-O-Rama*; Dramatists Guild Hull-Warriner Award for Best Play for *Spic-O-Rama*

1993   Theater World Award for Outstanding New Talent; Cable ACE for Best Writing, Entertainment Special for *HBO Comedy Hour: Spic-O-Rama*; Cable ACE for Best Performance in a Comedy Special for *HBO Comedy Hour: Spic-O-Rama*; Cable ACE for Best Comedy Special for *HBO Comedy Hour: Spic-O-Rama*

1998   Outer Critics Circle Award for Outstanding Solo Performance for *Freak*

1999   Drama Desk Award for Outstanding Solo/One-Person Show for *Freak*; Emmy Award for Outstanding Performance in a Variety or Music Program for *Freak*

FURTHER READING

Beane, Douglas Carter. "John Leguizamo: He's Got Legz." *Interview*, September 1995.

Brennan, Stephen, ed. *New Voices of the American Theater*. New York: Henry Holt, 1997.

Eaker, Sherry. "Leguizamo Debuts on Broadway." *Back Stage*, February 20, 1998.

Keller, Gary D. *A Biographical Handbook of Hispanics and United States Film*. Tempe, Ariz.: Bilingual Press, 1997.

Menard, Valerie. "In Latin Color: John Leguizamo's Variety Show, *House of Buggin'*, Puts Hispanics Back on Television." *Hispanic*, May 1995.

Rader, Dotson. "I Enjoy People Enjoying Me." *Parade*, July 25, 1999.

Reyes, Luis, and Peter Rubie. *Hispanics in Hollywood: A Celebration of 100 Years in Film and Television*. 2nd ed. New York: Garland, 2000.

Villela, Tony. "HBO Freaks on John Leguizamo." *Hispanic*, October 1998.

INDEX

ABOUT THE AUTHOR

AMY ALLISON's Spanish teacher at the University of California, Santa Barbara, hailed from Colombia, John Leguizamo's home country. Amy now lives in the Los Angeles area with her husband, Dave Edison. Other biographies she's written for Chelsea House include *Antonio Banderas*, also in the Latinos in the Limelight series. *The School Library Journal* called her book *Shakespeare's Globe* "an engaging read" and "a valuable resource for Shakespeare buffs." She is a Shakespeare fan and lists *Romeo and Juliet* as her favorite John Leguizamo movie.
